Praise for The Au k

"Kudos to Catherine Pascuas for sharing all she's learned from her unique perspective in life and from hosting The Autism Show podcast and giving us a simple, easy to use, effective toolbox with The Autism Activities Handbook. Catherine Pascuas "gets" that one size does not fit all. I found many useful, real tools and exercises that will help many on the spectrum, their teachers, and their loving families. Kudos to the author!"

- **Hackie Reitman, MD, neurodiversity advocate, author of Aspertools**

"We love this book which is choc-full of practical, simple games to engage your autistic child and help them with their development. They are realistic, a lot of fun and best of all - free!"

- **Debby Elley, co-editor AuKids magazine**

"The Autism Activities Handbook is a great tool for parents of young children with Autism Spectrum Disorder. The author has done a great job of compiling fun things any parent can do with their child to connect and help their children communicate. After my son received his ASD diagnosis I felt lost, I longed for a manual that would teach me how to play with him and help us both to be able to communicate with each other. When we started ABA, our therapists seemed to have an endless supply of games and activities that kept my child happy, learning and communicating. I longed to know the secret of how they got that level of interaction with my son. Catherine's book puts all of those tools in a parent's hands and she even includes great tips so that each activity can be modified to meet the individual child's needs. Even better, the book is formatted so you can start doing activities today, without having to read it cover to cover!"

– **Shannon Penrod, host of Autism Live**

"The Autism Activities Handbook is extremely user friendly. The author lays the foundation for the book by discussing the developmental and communicative stages so that the reader can easily identify the appropriate activities for any specific child. She expands this foundation by giving examples of adaptations for each activity. Every activity is easy to implement, yet geared toward a clearly stated purpose which will be helpful to educators working on specific goals. The easy-to-read format of bullet points will be a time saver for the user. A quick glance will alert the reader to the materials needed and the exact steps to follow for a successful, fun teaching session. Through her show, Ms. Pascuas has her finger on the pulse of the autism community and she has used that knowledge to create a book that should be on the bookshelf for every classroom and therapy room."

- **Dr. Linda Barboa, founder, Stars for Autism, Inc.**

"I am a homeschooling mom of two children who are living with autism. Keeping them active and learning throughout the day keeps me on my toes. As we have our children evaluated by professionals they may tell us, "your child has trouble with joint attention" or "we need to work on building core strength. " Having a resource like this would be great for both professionals and parents as a sort of quick reference guide to exercises and games to help build these skills. For professionals, rather than sending the parent away without tools to use at home, they could recommend this book to the family as resource. For a family, this is easy to read and the activities look like a lot fun. I will be trying them out in our home, for sure."

- **Shelli Allen, president of Steps Care Inc.**

"An amazing all-in-one guide of many crucial developmental skills for children with autism. This Handbook should be given to every parent of a child with autism along with university student therapists. Fun, meaningful activities are organized with step-by-step materials, procedures, alternatives, and rationales. Catherine's time and effort to share her expertise will change the lives of countless children with autism and their families."

- Karen Kabaki-Sisto, M.S. CCC-SLP, inventor of the iPad app I Can Have Conversations With You!™

“This book is filled with valuable activities to help children with autism learn and assist them in the development of their language skills, as well as their social and life skills. And it is done all through play; a perfect way to engage children while learning. It is designed so that people can easily access the activities they want and adapt them to the child’s specific needs. It is a perfect resource to have when working with children with Autism.”

- **Linda Mastroianni, Certified Life Coach/Autism Consultant, SpeakingAutism.ca**

“This book is full of playful and engaging interventions that professionals and parents can implement with children affected by Autism Spectrum Disorder. The interventions address the myriad of issues that children on the spectrum struggle with including communication skills, social skills, emotional regulation, life skills, motor issues, and anxiety struggles. Each intervention is clearly presented, low prop based, and easy to understand and implement. Professionals and parents will love having this resource of thoughtful interventions to address the needs of this very special population.”

- **Dr. Robert Jason Grant – author and creator of AutPlay® Therapy**

“As the parent of an adult son on the spectrum who struggled with midline, gross and small motor skills challenges, visual processing issues and challenges with depth perception, a book like this would have been extremely helpful. These activities not only are adaptable to each child's skill set, but crystallize transferable skills as well through the use of objects that the child uses in day to day life.”

- **Mari Nosal M.Ed.**

"It's such a pleasure to find a book that offers a treasure of practical, therapeutic, and easily-implemented activities that target an array of developmental skills. Strategies and ideas add a wealth of knowledge to enrich the lives of children through meaningful activity. What an asset to any home, classroom, or therapeutic setting!"

- **Lauren Brukner, MS, OTR/L, author and pediatric occupational therapist**

The Autism Activities Handbook:

Activities to Help Kids Communicate, Make Friends, and Learn Life Skills

Catherine Pascuas

Edx Autism Consulting

www.autismhandbooks.com

Illustrations by Robert Bull

The information presented in this book is educational and should not be construed as offering diagnostic, treatment, legal advice or consultation. If professional assistance in any of these areas is needed, the services of a competent autism professional should be sought.

Visit the author's website; comments and new ideas are welcome!

www.autismshow.org ; catherine@edxautism.com

ISBN 978 0 9951576 0 6

eISBN 978 0 9951576 1 3

Table of Contents

Foreword

It was a bright sunny day in Pennsylvania. The new beginnings of spring were in the air. However, as my son and I walked out of the developmental pediatrician's office, I felt only darkness and gloom. That was the day my son was diagnosed with autism.

Nothing prepares a parent for the complicated challenges autism brings. As a mother of two children with autism, I can relate. I consistently search for books and resources to help my sons. When a parent has a tool that provides guidance, the future becomes brighter. Hope outshines darkness and excitement replaces anxiety. I enjoy writing books such as, The Parent's Guide to Occupational Therapy for Autism and The Special Needs School Survival Guide book in order to give strategies and guidance to families of children with autism. When I provide activities that I have trialed with my own children and clients, I feel confident in recommending them to my readers.

Catherine Pascuas brings unique skills to the table. I personally know how passionate she is about helping children with autism. Her weekly podcast, The Autism Show, allows leading autism advocates, educators, professionals, and organizations to share their inspirational stories and best resources with the global autism community. As a behavior specialist, Catherine founded Edx Autism Consulting. She understands the information parents need and how to present it in a way that appeals to her readers. Catherine has assembled a team of experts in autism in order to bring you the most up to date techniques. Behavior specialists grasp the importance of training families. When a caregiver feels empowered, excitement builds and becomes contagious! Children have fun while learning. Catherine understands the need for children to learn and improve by enhancing their knowledge and experience for the hurdles ahead.

Throughout this book there are activities which will not only engage children but teach critical skills needed for function. As an occupational therapist I know that children learn through playing. The Autism Activities Handbook packs in activities for communication, life skills, coordination, and sensory processing, among many others. It is a comprehensive and engaging book which you will refer to over and over. One of my favorite activities is 'Getting Ready for a Playdate.' Social gatherings often cause great anxiety among children and parents. Catherine provides step by step directions to guide readers. The 'Making a Fidget' activity gives tips for sensory activity that children will enjoy and use over and over again.

Every time you pick up this book, you will find a creative and well-planned activity that will help build skills for a lifetime. I'm very excited about this book and promise you will find it to be an invaluable resource.

Cara Koscinski, MOT, OTR/L

Founder of The Pocket Occupational Therapist
Award-Winning Author: The Parents Guide to Occupational Therapy for Autism,
The Weighted Blanket Guide, and the Special Needs School Survival Guide
Charleston, SC

Introduction

This book is for you if you are a parent of a child on the autism spectrum or if you work with children on the autism spectrum as a caregiver, therapist, or teacher.

In the last seven years, working one-on-one with kids on the autism spectrum and their families, I've seen the need for simple and easy activities and games to keep kids occupied and learning at the same time. After all, the best way to learn is through play.

However, I'm no expert. Most of the ideas in this book come from brilliant minds and true experts who have shared some of their ideas.

I especially hope this book will be a valuable resource for your family. The book contains easy-to-implement games and activities that your child can play, resulting in developmental growth in language, social skills, and life skills.

Each game is adaptable to best meet children's needs, no matter their developmental stage or age.

Enjoy!

"We have got to work on keeping these children engaged with the world."

Dr Temple Grandin, autism activist

How to use this book

As a parent, caregiver, therapist, or teacher, you're busy with the daily grind. Yet you still want to help your child on the autism spectrum learn and grow. This book has been written and organized in a simple manner, so you don't have to read the entire book. Rather, you can collect tidbits of information that you need as you go along to help your child develop language, social skills, and life skills while they have fun.

Here are four rules to follow:

1. Don't read this book from start to finish. You may have heard the now infamous saying that "if you know one child with autism, you know one child with autism." This means not everything in this book will apply to your child (or the child you're working with). It also means you'll get to pick and choose which activities from the book best apply to your child. To select an activity based on a goal or skill your child is working on, you can browse the table of contents and find the chapters that are most relevant. Once you've chosen an activity, get started.

2. Share this book. If you are a parent, share this book with your child's teachers, tutors, babysitters, and others. Often, people working with kids on the spectrum run out of ideas and fun activities to keep children engaged.

These creative games and activities will keep a child entertained for hours while helping them learn and improve their developmental skill set.

3. This book will evolve with your feedback and help. If you find mistakes or have ideas to share, please send your feedback to catherine@edxautism.com.

4. Have fun! This book is meant to get you interacting with your child. Remember to have fun, which is an integral part of learning.

Acknowledgements

First, I must thank all podcast guests from The Autism Show. I've learned so much from your insights on and off the air.

Robert Bull, thank you for your wonderful illustrations. Keep drawing. Thanks to your sister, Andrea Bull, for her willingness to help out and collaborate when this book was still a tiny idea.

To all the people who trusted this project with their credit cards and backed the Kickstarter campaign for The Autism Activities Handbook: This project couldn't have happened without each and every one of you.

To all the families that I have worked with, your dedication and commitment are a true inspiration.

And last, to my cousin, Alex, who is my biggest source of inspiration.

Your Gift

Special Offer – 12 more activities and games!

Learning doesn't have to be boring! Help your kids learn social skills with ideas for play dates.

Take advantage of this free social skills activities builder pdf offer. Visit us online at AutismHandbooks.com to download these activities right now with special offers and bonus content.

Chapter 1: Communication

Kids on the autism spectrum and those with other conditions may have delayed communication skills. How do you know your child's communication level?

Stage 1 — No deliberate communication; reacting to feelings and situations

Examples: crying, facial expressions, body movements, smiling, and basic vocal sounds

Stage 2 — Sending nonverbal messages with a deliberate purpose using gestures and/or sounds

This could be communication to get your attention. At this stage, joint attention is possible. The child begins to understand certain words and phrases and can follow basic directions. Once a child understands what certain words mean, verbal communication can follow.

Stage 3 — Using basic vocabulary to express the names of people, objects, or actions

Speech is limited to single words to express an idea. For example, a child may say "Dada" when pointing to Dad's chair. At this stage, some words may be difficult to understand if a child uses a short version, such as nana for banana.

Stage 4 — Two-word phrases

At this stage, children ask questions by changing their tone of voice and, they use phrases, such as "Where mommy?"

The activities in this book will mostly help kids in Stages 3 and 4.

Now that you know more about your child's communication level, you can move on to the activities in this chapter.

Let the fun begin!

Finish the song (imitations and interactions)

This activity is designed for children who may have difficulties with spontaneous speech or who are less verbal. This engaging and interactive activity will help the child initiate speech using familiar songs. You may want to brush up on your nursery rhymes and singing before trying out this activity.

Materials

- Child's preferred activity toy, such as a swing, large exercise ball, or small trampoline

Steps

1. Engage the child in the preferred activity, such as swinging on a swing, bouncing on a large exercise ball, or jumping on a small trampoline.
2. Continue the activity while singing a children's tune such as the ABCs or "Row, Row, Row Your Boat."
3. When the child is engaged, leave the ending of the song unsung.
4. Wait for the child to finish the ending of the song.
5. Repeat this several times.
6. Try this exercise with more songs or rhymes. Notice if the child takes a particular interest in a certain song.

Alternatives

If your child is older or not interested in nursery rhymes, you can try singing popular music your child may know.

Learning new words (building vocabulary)

Vocabularies shape the way we think and learn about the world. A varied vocabulary is needed to excel in school; further, building children's vocabulary helps them develop language and literacy skills. Parents and educators should stay one step ahead of the child by modeling words and concepts that are slightly beyond the child's level of understanding. This will help them learn new vocabulary. It's not only about what you say but how you say it.

Materials

- None

Steps

1. Talk about things that interest your child. Follow your child's lead (this makes it more likely they will pay attention to your words).
2. Provide explanations. Past the infant stage, you can begin to use more expansive vocabulary. Talk about future events, such as needing to go to the car wash because the car is dirty. Talk about events in the past ("Remember when the cars crashed?").

3. Wait and listen. Don't bombard the child with constant chatter. Give your child a chance to respond by pausing after you say something.
4. Model words with actions. Use appropriate facial expressions, gestures, and actions to give strong visual cues to your child. This will help them learn and understand the meaning of new words. For example, you can yawn or lie down when explaining the word exhausted.
5. Repeat, repeat, repeat. Repeat the same word for your child on different occasions. Most children must understand a word's meaning before saying the word.
6. Be a human dictionary. When using new vocabulary, provide a simple definition of the word so your child can understand what the new word means. If you include your child in the context, it will be easier for your child to understand the meaning of the new word. For example, if you are explaining the word anxious to your child, you might say, "Remember your birthday party, and how you felt anxious? But eventually you felt comfortable around your new friends, and you didn't feel anxious anymore."

Alternatives

If you have a young infant who enjoys playing with toy cars, you might use words like beep beep or crash. With a toddler or older child, you might use more advanced words, like mechanic or traffic.

Using bubbles to further communication (talking in sentences)

Bubbles. Some kids can spend hours making and popping bubbles. Bubbles are a great inexpensive, interactive activity to help your child participate in verbal and nonverbal play. Here, we use bubbles to encourage the child to communicate and interact with you or other children. By using bubble play, you can create an environment to encourage your child to send you messages — "More bubbles!"

Materials

- Bubble wands
- Bubble solution, purchased or homemade (recipe: mix 1 part dish soap with 3 parts water; add a couple teaspoons of sugar)

Steps

1. Get face-to-face with the child. By being at the child's level, it's easier to encourage interaction.
2. Introduce the activity. Say something like "It's time to blow bubbles."
3. Start blowing bubbles. Pause and wait for the child to communicate, indicating more bubbles. This can be in the form of a word or sign: eye contact, pointing to the bubble solution, or

reaching for the wand.*

4. Blow more bubbles. Pause again to wait for more communication from the child.

*If the child is having difficulty communicating, you can incorporate a cue to help the child send a message. For example, lean in close to the child, look expectantly, and say the first sound of the word. If this doesn't work, you can say a word or short sentence that the child can copy.

Alternatives

You can use this game during a playdate. If the child can speak in sentences, encourage the child to make longer comments, such as "Wow! That's a big bubble!" or "You caught it!" Then wait for the child to make comments, too. If the child needs help, say something to start the sentence: "Look, that bubble ... " Then wait for the child to finish the sentence.

Squish! (talking in sentences)

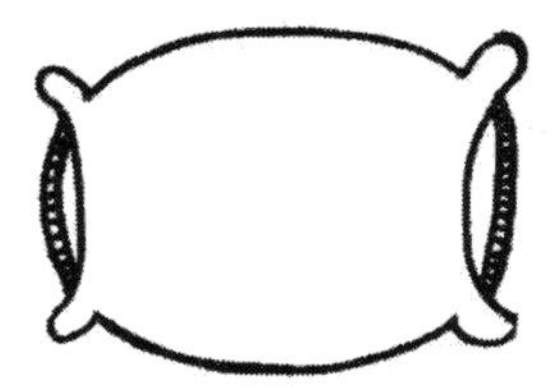

Many children I have worked with enjoy the sensation of deep pressure. Being squished gently by hugs or cushions can be a calming and rewarding experience for children. Deep pressure can be a great motivation to get children talking in sentences.

Materials

- Sofa cushions or pillows

Steps

1. Have the child lie on a sofa and mention that you are going to squish him with the cushion or pillow.
2. Use one of the sofa cushions or pillows to gently squish the child's torso or arm. Apply gentle pressure. If the child enjoys the sensation, you can apply pressure for up to 10 seconds.

3. Encourage the child to say a short sentence, such as "Squish me!" or "More Squish!" or a longer three-word sentence, such as "More squish, please." Bring your face down to eye level to give the child a chance to ask using eye contact. Give a helpful prompt if the child needs help. Apply another deep pressure squish once the child asks.
4. Take turns and have the child try squishing you!

Masked characters (asking/answering personal questions)

Many kids enjoy dressing up or playing their favorite characters. This game is especially great if your child is interested in cartoon characters. This game helps them practice communication and interaction while asking and answering personal questions. It's a great way to practice taking an interest in others.

Materials

- Internet connection
- Printer
- Paper
- Pen or pencil
- 2 chairs

Steps

Prep

1. Search online for images of cartoon characters.
2. Print out the images of the child's favorite cartoon characters. (You can glue the cartoon face image on a stick to hold up to your face or simply hold up the printed image over your face.)

3. Sit down with the child and come up with several questions to ask the cartoon characters, such as "What is your name?" or "Who is your friend?" You may want to write out the questions so the child can remember.

The interview

1. Set up two chairs across from each other; the child sits on one, and you sit on the other.
2. Hold up a printed cartoon image and tell the child to pretend you are the cartoon character.
3. Allow the child to ask the cartoon character several questions.
4. Repeat the interview process for all the characters, taking turns with the child as the cartoon character.

Food monster (asking/answering "what" questions)

Being silly can help keep children motivated during an activity. In this game, children learn and practice how to ask and answer "what" questions, while you get to eat a snack. It's a win-win situation!

Materials

- 3 plates with different bite-sized food items on each (pieces of fruit, nuts, small chocolates)
- Fork

Steps

1. Sit at a table with the child. Have three plates of food set up.
2. Tell the child to help feed you.
3. Instruct the child to ask, "What do you want to eat?"
4. Give an answer and have the child pick up the food item with a fork and feed you. Make sure you give a silly or animated monster face while you eat to engage the child.
5. Each time you finish a bite, ask the child to repeat the question, "What do you want to eat?"
6. Continue taking turns being the food monster until you have finished the food.

Alternatives

This is a great game to play during snack time, with a playdate, or with siblings. Once the child understands the game, you can increase the number of food plates on the table.

Memory card game (advanced communication)

A turn-taking game is a great way to help kids learn advanced communication skills. What better way to learn taking turns than with a memory card game — the same one you played as a kid. This game helps children make simple descriptive sentences.

Materials

- Memory card game (premade cards or make your own with duplicate pictures)

Steps

1. Start with two pairs of cards (once the child's skills increase, you can add additional pairs).
2. Place cards facedown in a grid pattern.

3. Instruct the child to pick up two cards. If the two cards match, have the child make a sentence. For example, if two lions are matched, the child can say, “A big lion sleeps in a cave.” If the cards don’t match, return them to the facedown position.
4. Take turns.

How do I feel? (expressing emotive information)

Kids need an outlet to express their emotions. Introducing them to journaling is a great way to help them initiate emotional expression. This game is great for older children who understand full sentences.

Materials

- Notebook
- Marker, pen, or pencil

Steps

1. Have the child decorate and place their name on the cover of a notebook.
2. Mention you will be writing in your journal at the end of the day, and the child will be writing in his journal at the end of the day, as well.
3. At the end of the day (or at the end of a session), encourage the child to write a sentence or two about their emotions that day. For example, the child may write, "I was angry when Tommy took my book," or "I was happy there was no school today."
4. You can also have the child draw a picture to represent the written feelings.

5. Create a schedule (for example, once a day or three times a week) for your child to write in the journal.

Alternatives

If the child finds it challenging to come up with an emotion to write about, you can help by listing different emotions on a journal page.

Theater speak (intonation)

Some children (and adults) on the spectrum excel at theater performance. This simple theater activity will help your child use different intonations — particularly helpful if the child tends to use a monotone voice.

Materials

- Internet connection (to find a short two-character script)
- Props or costumes

Steps

1. Find a developmentally appropriate (simple, short) script online for two people (or write your own).
2. Read the play to the child and have the child choose a character to play.
3. Have the child pick out the appropriate costumes or props.
4. Practice reading the play together and instruct the child to use their voice to show different emotions of the character.
5. Repeat the play several times until the child begins to use different intonations to portray the character. Then perform in front of family members.

Insect photo sharing (advanced communication)

Use this fun interactive game to take turns talking and listening with your child. This is for children who can have simple back-and-forth conversations. All you need is a digital camera (or your picture-taking smartphone).

Many children find insects interesting; this game is a great way to spend time in nature and learn about insects. If your child is afraid or uninterested in the insect world, you can easily substitute other interesting things you find on a nature walk, such as trees or leaves.

Materials

- Digital camera or picture-taking device

Steps

1. Go on a short neighborhood walk and take pictures of things you or your child finds interesting. For example, you might find an interesting ladybug and the child might find an ant.
2. After the nature walk, look at the pictures.
3. Take turns explaining to each other what insect is in the picture, what you know about this insect (where the head is, its body color, and so on), and why you think this insect is interesting.

Alternatives

Try taking pictures of interesting things in different settings. For example, take pictures of different items you find at a grocery store or of different animals at a zoo.

Joint attention (advanced communication)

Joint attention, imitation, and pretend play are incredibly important for communication and social interaction. By targeting these important skills early, we stack the odds in kids' favor for better communication outcomes.

You can help your child develop these skills. Remember to follow your child's lead by paying attention to their interests and noticing what toys or activities the child engages with. By joining the fun with the child, you are setting the stage for advanced communication.

Materials

- None

Steps

1. Look at and talk about what the child is interested in at the moment.

   For example, if your child likes cars, you might look at your daily routines and find that the following activities involve cars:

   - riding in the car each day on the way to daycare
   - going to the car wash
   - filling the car up with gas

- reading books about cars
- playing with cars during playtime

1. Sit on the floor or kneel at the child's level.
2. Talk about what the child is playing with or looking at. Make a comment, such as "Wow, that's a fast car!"
3. Join in by copying what the child is doing.
4. Once the child is paying attention, add a related action and see if the child imitates what you are doing. For example, if the child is playing with a toy kitchen, initially imitate what the child is doing and then try doing something different, such as using the pots in the toy kitchen.
5. Encourage the child to imitate your actions and keep the game going back and forth.

Speaking intentionally (advanced communication)

Some children on the spectrum may have a hard time using intentional communication, which is sending messages with the purpose of attaining a specific goal (example: directly asking for a cookie). When a child's messages are indirect (part of early communication), understanding the message can be difficult. To build a communicative relationship with your child, begin by trying to understand the message. This activity encourages interaction and provides opportunities for your child to direct a message to you.

Materials

- Paper and pen for taking notes

Steps

1. Get down at the child's eye level and pay attention to the child's focus and interests. When you are face-to-face, it's easier for your child to look at you and communicate.
2. Keep a list of sounds and noises your child makes during certain situations. Also note what you think the sounds mean and what your child is trying to communicate.
3. Say and do something that matches the meaning behind your child's message. This helps the child make the connection that behavior has meaning. For example, you can interpret your child's messages when he looks at cookies on the table and makes a sound, or smiles when he sees and hears a favorite musical toy. You can say, "Mmmm ... cookies!" or "You want a cookie" and give a cookie to the child. You can hold up the musical toy and say, "You like the music" or "Nice music!"
4. Encourage your child to send messages for activities that have a clear goal, such as receiving a snack, jumping on a trampoline, receiving a tickle, and so on.

5. Pause and wait for your child to communicate directly with you. For example, you might help your child jump on the trampoline. Then encourage him to say "jump" or a longer sentence before you help him jump again.
6. Be sure to follow your child's lead. Use activities your child likes and stop once interest wanes.

Chapter 2: Social skills

"Social thinking skills must be directly taught to children and adults with ASD. Doing so opens doors of social understandings in all areas of life."

Dr Temple Grandin

What are social skills?

Social skills involve one or more of the following:

- Friendship skills — making and keeping friends, dealing with peer pressure
- Emotional skills — self-regulation of emotions, reading facial expressions and body language
- Play skills — pretend and imaginative play, playing with others, taking turns, coping with losing, dealing with conflict
- Conversation skills — greetings, joining a conversation, awareness of personal space, ending a conversation

In what areas do kids with autism have difficulties?

Children on the autism spectrum often have difficulty with social interaction, verbal and nonverbal communication with others, and imaginative play. Teaching your child social skills opens up opportunities for your child to engage in the community as well as to make friends.

Typically, social skills come naturally with basic guidance. For kids on the spectrum or with similar conditions, more effort is required to learn the social skills needed to navigate society.

Many kids on the spectrum can feel overwhelmed by social interactions with peers. Help your child practice social skills in safe situations, and simplify social rules, explaining them at a pace a child with autism understands.

The activities and games in this chapter offer practical ideas to help kids develop social skills.

Where am I looking? (eye contact)

Eye contact shows we are interested and listening to what other people are communicating. This game teaches how eye contact draws attention. Your child learns to track your eyes to see where your attention is focused.

Materials

- 10 pictures of objects or characters that fascinate your child
- Tape

Steps

1. Tape ten pictures on the walls of the room.
2. Instruct the child to stand on one side of the room and to look at only one of the pictures.
3. Follow the child's eyes to guess which picture the child has chosen.
4. If the guess is correct, take the picture down.
5. Now it's your turn. Allow the child to guess where you are looking and to choose the correct picture.
6. Continue the game until all the pictures have been taken down.

Alternatives

For younger children, you can use these ideas to increase spontaneous eye contact through nonverbal praise:

1. Funny glasses — Wearing silly glasses may encourage the child to look at your eyes.
2. Squeeze or tickle — Give the child a small squeeze or short tickle (if they enjoy this) as a nonverbal reinforcement.
3. Staring contest — Engage in a staring contest with the child. Whoever holds eye contact longest wins.
4. Eye stickers — Place two stickers just above your eyebrows. Encourage the child to look at the stickers when engaging in a short conversation. This won't be direct eye contact but will encourage looking in the right direction.

Follow my voice (following directions)

Kids on the spectrum often have a difficult time following directions. This game is similar to the game Simon Says. The idea is to help kids understand by listening rather than using visual clues. This game can be quite challenging. It targets auditory processing, following directions, and impulse control. You can play this game with the child or with a group at school, in social programs, or even during a playdate.

Materials

- Colored pieces of paper or colored mats

Steps

1. Lay the colored paper or mats on the ground and have the children spread out around them.
2. Instruct the children to look at you while you give directions.
3. Hold up a certain colored paper or mat while giving the instruction to move to another colored paper or mat. For example, say, "Go to the green square" while holding up a blue square.
4. Have the children take turns being the leader.

Alternatives

If the original version of the game is too challenging, try this simple version:

- Give the instruction to copy your actions but to ignore any directions you say out loud.
- Instruct the children to do an action while you do a completely different action. For example, instruct the group to jump on the spot while patting your head. (The correct action would be for the group to follow your verbal command of jumping on the spot.)

The action rock game (taking turns)

Turn-taking skills are incredibly important for youngsters to learn as part of early social skills development. Using movement (motor skills) is a great way to learn turn-taking skills while having fun. This game is quick, easy to set up, and can be played with a group of kids at school or during playdates at home. Encourage the child to make different variations of the game to learn more skills.

Materials

- Sidewalk chalk
- A paved outdoor area
- A small rock

Steps

1. Draw a large game board on the ground with the chalk, similar to a tic-tac-toe grid.
2. Write or draw instructions on each square. Kids can help with this step or decorate the squares.
3. Include instructions using motor skills on each square, such as jump on the spot 2 times, hop on one foot 4 times, touch your toes 3 times, spin around on the spot 2 times, and so on.
4. Have the child throw a rock onto the board to move ahead.

5. The child must complete the action on the square that the rock lands on before the next player takes a turn.
6. Encourage the child to keep track of whose turn it is.

Alternatives

In addition to motor skills, you can use the same game board to help the child learn letters, numbers, and math problems. For example, you can write addition, subtraction, division, and multiplication problems suited to the child's skill level and age on the game board.

Getting ready for a playdate (playing with friends and siblings)

Playdates can be a challenge for kids on the spectrum unless you have a plan of action. Follow this guide to set up a successful playdate. For younger children especially, attention spans can be limited, so have between three to five activities planned for an hour playdate. Take time to familiarize the child on the spectrum with a specific game. For example, if you'll be playing a board game during the playdate, have the child play this game several times before the playdate to get to know the rules of the game. This will give the child a fair chance to process what's going on before interacting with other children.

Limit the playdate to one peer. Interactions can be overwhelming for kids on the spectrum, so allow the child to practice playdate routines with only one other child before you move on to group playdates.

Sometimes, you may need to step in to keep interactions between the kids positive but allow some interactions to occur naturally. You want the child to have a good time and have a positive memory of the playdate, so remember to keep it simple and fun!

Steps

1. Plan ahead — Think about what skills your child excels at. If your child enjoys playing with Lego or drawing, that's a good place to start a playdate interaction. It also helps to know ahead of time what the peer is interested in. If you can find a match in preferences, that's perfect!
2. Keep it short — It's easier to keep kids engaged for shorter periods of time.
3. Plan for an ending — Don't forget to prepare the child for the end of a playdate. Practice by using a five-minute countdown timer to announce the playdate will end soon. Have a reward or incentive waiting for the child for saying or otherwise expressing goodbye as the friend leaves.

Here's a sample playdate timeline:

- First 10 minutes — free play time; kids have a choice for their own preferred activity
- Next 10 minutes — facilitated play (for example, a board game)
- 15 minutes — snack time
- 10 minutes — facilitated play
- 10 minutes — outdoor play or another facilitated game
- Last 5 minutes — countdown

More tips for a successful playdate:

- Adults can forget how children play. Don't let your adult preconceptions interfere with the kids' interactions.
- Keep your assistance to a minimum and try not to embarrass the child by correcting their actions in front of their peers.
- Stay observant. Pay close attention to the child's social behaviors while they play. This gives you the opportunity to identify social skills for the child to practice.

Belly breaths (starting a playdate with exercise)

Starting a playdate with simple breathing exercises can be a good warm-up and can help children feel calm before a playdate. These exercises help relieve anxiety and stress, as well as help release uncomfortable emotions that are common in kids on the autism spectrum.

Bringing an awareness to breathing helps children develop self-regulation or self-soothing and can be a good coping strategy if the child has social anxiety.

Have the children do this exercise together before you begin any activities that require more interaction. Taking deep breaths or doing yoga poses at the start of a playdate helps the children focus.

Materials

- None

Steps

1. Sit on the floor and have the children sit on the floor facing you.
2. Ask the kids to mirror your actions. To help the kids visualize the proper breathing technique, tell them to make their bellies full of air when they inhale.

3. Breathe in through the nose slowly and fill up your lungs.
4. Hold the breath for a count of five.
5. Slowly release the breath from the mouth.
6. Repeat belly breaths five times.
7. Remind the kids that these belly breaths are a good exercise and strategy to use if they get upset.

Beanbag and basket toss (educational playdate activity)

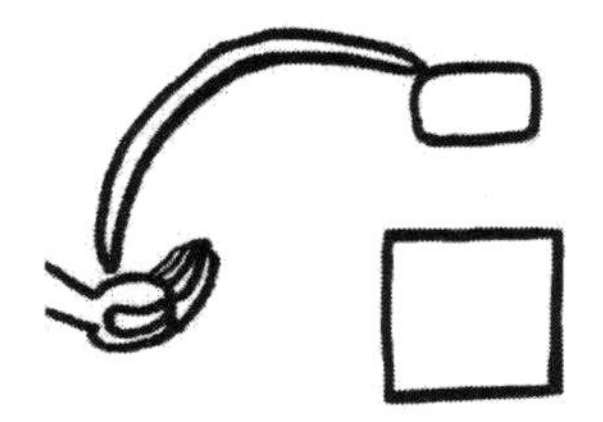

Playdates are a wonderful time to play educational games while practicing taking turns and social skills. In this activity, you ask the kids questions (related to school work or math drills, for example) while they play basket toss. Who said educational games have to be boring?

Materials

- Beanbags (or small stuffed toys)
- Small baskets (or similar-sized containers)

Steps

1. Place the basket on the floor a few steps away from the kids.

2. Pick a topic for questions — homework questions or math drills such as addition or multiplication. You may want to write the questions on a piece of paper so you can easily refer to them during the game.
3. Each child takes a turn answering questions. A correct answer wins a beanbag toss.
4. Award one point for each correct answer and one point for each beanbag that lands in the basket. The child with the most points at the end of the game wins.

Puppet play (creative playdate activity)

Children on the autism spectrum are often overloaded with structured routines and drills at school and even in home therapy sessions. Playing with puppets breaks this structured routine by fostering creativity and imaginary play, helping the child develop abstract thinking and ideas. You can do this activity one-on-one with the child or during a playdate.

Materials

- Puppets or stuffed animals

Steps

1. Have the children sit on the floor with the puppets.
2. Encourage the children to make a puppet show. You may need to facilitate the play and let the children follow your lead. Once the children are familiar with the idea of a puppet show, they can create their own puppet show ideas.

Here are some puppet show ideas to get you started:

- Dining out — Have the puppets order food at a pretend restaurant and then eat.
- Birthday — Pretend it's one of the puppet's birthdays. Have all the puppets sit at a table and sing "“Happy Birthday." Have the birthday puppet blow out the candles on a pretend cake.

- Bedtime — Have the puppets go through a bedtime routine, including putting on their pjs, brushing their teeth, and so on.
- Biting — Have an animal puppet pretend to bite the child. Give the animal puppet a timeout and have the animal apologize.
- Cheer up — Have the puppets cheer up the sad puppet.
- School — Have the puppets pretend to be in school and assign one puppet as the teacher.

Alternatives

For children who may have a hard time with abstract thinking or imagination, find short, simple scripts online for children to follow. Make sure scripts are developmentally appropriate.

Whiteboard faces (emotional recognition)

Some kids on the spectrum have difficulties recognizing subtle facial emotional responses. This game helps the child practice facial recognition and emotional intelligence in a fun way. Understanding the nuances of facial features helps children understand other people's emotions and reactions and is part of social skills development.

Materials

- Whiteboard
- Whiteboard markers

Steps

1. Draw a face with a missing facial feature (for example, leave out a smile, an eye, or an eyebrow).

2. Label the image with an emotion, such as anger, sadness, or happiness.
3. Have the child fill in the missing parts of the face.

Alternatives

Depending on the child's developmental level, adjust the level of difficulty by having your child look for clues about the emotion. For example, if the child is advanced, have the child ask questions about what the face is feeling or what type of situation would make the face feel the emotion.

If the child is at an introductory level, draw the entire face and have the child label the emotion.

The feeling jar (sharing emotions and feelings)

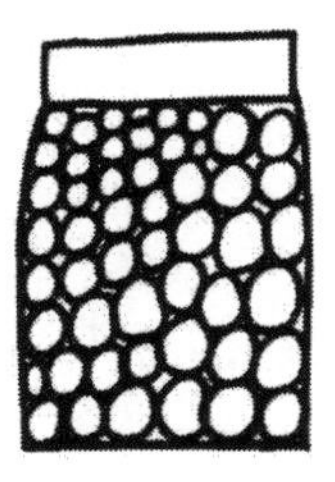

Sometimes kids have a hard time expressing their feelings — especially kids on the autism spectrum. This game helps them sort through their emotions by using a visual helper and is great for helping kids with emotional expression and regulation.

Materials

- Differently colored pom-poms
- Clear jar

Steps

1. Have the child assign a feeling to each color of pom-pom. For example, blue can mean frustration and red can mean angry.

2. Have the child label the emotion they are feeling, pick the corresponding pom-pom, and place it in the jar.
3. Instruct the child to keep adding pom-poms for every different emotion they are feeling. For example, if they are having mixed feelings about the first day of school, they might choose a blue pom-pom for sad, a red one for feeling anxious or worried, and a green one for excited.
4. Mix all the pom-poms in the jar and explain to the child that it's normal to have a mix of feelings.
5. Ask which emotion is the biggest and tell them to add more of that pom-pom. For example, if they are mostly feeling anxious or worried about the first day of school, have the child add more red pom-poms to the jar.
6. If the jar is mainly filled with positive emotions, mention that it's okay to feel a little nervous or sad. If the jar is mainly filled with negative emotions, discuss with the child how to solve the problem or deal with these emotions.

Photoshoot connections (showing interest in others)

Taking interest in others is an important part of social development. This game helps your child learn details about their peers without the stress of one-on-one interactions. In this game, we let the camera do the talking. Let the connections begin!

Materials

- Digital camera or smartphone
- Paper
- 4 people

Steps

1. Encourage the child to help find four friends or family members who will let you take several pictures of them. You may need to facilitate the photoshoot depending on the child's communication level.
2. Take a picture of the first person and ask them to make a change for each of the next three photographs. For example, they might wear a hat in the second picture, change a facial expression in the second, and take off their socks in the third picture.

3. Repeat this picture-taking process with the three other people. You should have a total of four photographs for each person.
4. Print out all the pictures and put two pictures of the same person side by side. Glue these pictures on a piece of paper or print them out together on one page.
5. Present each page (with the two pictures) to the child.
6. Ask the child to name the differences between the two pictures on the page.
7. Repeat with the other sets of pictures.

Alternatives

If your child is having a hard time, you may want to find funny pictures of people your child recognizes, like family members.

Measuring-tape fun (showing interest in others)

I loved playing with a measuring tape from my mom's sewing kit when I was little. A measuring tape is a simple thing that can keep kids entertained for long periods of time. This game helps children take an interest in others — one of the first steps in social interaction. Put away the iPad and see how you measure up!

Materials

- Paper or poster board
- Pencil or pen
- Measuring tape

Steps

1. On a large piece of paper or poster board, write "Name" and then list five measurements: height, foot length, face length, index finger length, and thumb width.
2. Allow your child to come up with another three areas to measure and add them to the piece of paper.
3. Have the child take self-measurements and write down the numbers under the correct headings.

4. Have the child take measurements of peers or family members. You may need to facilitate these interactions depending on the child's level of communication.

Chapter 3: Life skills

"The ultimate goal of parents, educators, and professionals who interact with children with autism is to unlock their potential to become self-reliant, fully-integrated, contributing members of society. We have the power to unlock this potential by implementing an effectively structured intervention — that which takes the development of the whole child into account."

Dr Karina Poirier, Unlocking the Social Potential in Autism

It's important to help children on the autism spectrum develop practical life skills — including personal care — that foster independence in the home and community. The activities in this chapter offer engaging instruction and strategies for teaching these skills.

What are life skills?

Life skills include basic skills such as personal hygiene and safety, as well as tasks like cooking, cleaning, getting dressed, shopping, ordering at a restaurant, getting around, and making healthy choices. Some of these skills overlap with social skills.

Why is teaching life skills so important?

Greater independence leads to increased employment and living options for your child. Further, children who can do things themselves have higher self-esteem.

Scheduling life skills activities

Every family functions differently and on different schedules. There are no hard and fast rules about how often you should do these activities. Frequency depends on the child's abilities and the family's lifestyle.

Create your own daily and weekly routine to incorporate these activities. For example, try incorporating 15 to 20 minutes of these activities three times a week.

If you are a parent or caregiver, here are some things to consider when making a daily and weekly routine:

Think about times in the day you have 15 minutes to spare. Maybe it's in the afternoon after school or just before bedtime. Maybe you can take a 15-minute break during homework time.

Can you make any of these activities a regular part of family life?

Bite-sized guess (eating)

Mealtimes can be one of the most stressful parts of the day. Children on the autism spectrum are often considered picky eaters. Some children dislike foods with a certain feel, smell, or taste. This game helps children have fun while trying new foods. Try playing fun music just before and during mealtimes to help set the mood. If the child is feeling anxious about trying new foods, you can encourage the child to play games with food to help the child relax.

Materials

- Fruits and/or vegetables
- Plate
- Blindfold (optional)

Steps

1. Wash and dry the fruits and vegetables. Keep the fruit or vegetable whole.
2. Have the child wear a blindfold or close their eyes and try to identify each fruit or vegetable by touch. If the child is having trouble identifying the fruit or vegetable, give the child hints. You can limit the guesses to three before moving on to the next vegetable.

3. Once the child is ready to try the fruit or vegetable, cut it into bite-sized pieces and have the child try to identify the fruit by smell and then taste.

Alternatives

Give the child the whole fruit or vegetable inside an upside-down cardboard box with holes cut out for arms. Ask the child to feel the fruit or vegetable and guess which vegetable or fruit it is.

Chewy necklace (unwanted chewing)

Some children on the autism spectrum have a tendency to chew on inappropriate things, such as T-shirt sleeves or shirt collars. One child I knew had holes all over his clothing. In this activity, you'll help a child make an edible necklace they can chew on.

Materials

- Thin string or elastic string
- Cereal with holes (donut-shaped cereal)
- Scissors

Steps

1. Cut the elastic string to make a necklace that hangs at least three inches from the child's collarbone.
2. Tie a large knot in one end of the string.

3. String pieces of cereal, adding more pieces until the necklace is full.
4. Tie the ends of the string together.

Alternatives

Make an edible bracelet if the child doesn't want a necklace.

Making a fidget (emotional regulation)

Fidgets help a child self-soothe instead of melting down. (Note: It's best to do this activity when the child is calm.) Making this glitter jar helps children regulate their emotions when they feel stress or anxiety. When making the jar, you'll engage the child in a discussion about feelings to help them express their emotions. Once the fidget jar is complete, place it in an accessible area, ready whenever the child needs to calm down.

Materials

- Vegetable oil
- Food coloring
- Water
- Colored glitter
- Clear jar
- Marker

Steps

1. Ask the child about feeling happy or content. Ask them to choose a glitter color that matches that feeling.
2. Ask the child about feeling upset. Have them choose a color of food coloring to match this feeling. Add one or two drops to water in a jar.
3. Mix all the ingredients (colored glitter and a small amount of vegetable oil) in the jar with water.

4. Seal the jar, shake the jar gently, and watch the oil and water mix and then separate.

Focus obstacle course (focus and attention)

Focusing and paying attention is often a big challenge for kids on the autism spectrum. For younger children, working on step-by-step activities can help organize the brain for a focused task. This activity helps kids organize their brain using an obstacle course. It's best to play this game before the child sits down to do an activity that requires focus. In this game, children must focus their attention to remember the instructions for an obstacle course.

Materials

- Household materials
- A room, hallway, or open space

Steps

1. Create a small obstacle course using different household materials. For example, you might set up two chairs, a table, and a several pots and pans on the floor. You can have the child help set up the obstacle course.
2. Give the child specific instructions to remember to complete the obstacle course.

Here's a sample obstacle course:

- Go around the first chair twice.

- Crawl under the table.
- Sit on the second chair for five seconds.
- Dance around the pots and pans.

Alternatives

To facilitate participation, have the child draw out a simple map of the obstacle course on a piece of paper, including the household materials.

With older children, getting ready for an activity that requires focus may require a more calm activity, such as a crossword puzzle or logic puzzle.

Exercises for anxiety (regulating feelings of anxiety)

For kids with social anxiety, large groups can be a trigger. Exercise with large muscle groups reduces anxiety. Next time your child gets anxious about a large group setting, set aside time for these exercises beforehand.

Materials

- Wall (optional)
- Heavy object (optional)

Steps

Instruct the child to take part in one or several of the following exercises for a few minutes before entering an anxiety-triggering social situation.

1. Jumping on the spot
2. Performing push-ups against a wall
3. Carrying a heavy object or heavy ball around the room

Fishing fun (movement)

Try this simple fishing game to help your child work on gross motor skills. You'll need some online pictures.

Materials

- Fish made out of paper or light cardboard (about 2 inches or 5 cm in length)
- Paper clips
- Small, flat magnets
- Crafted fishing pole (a dowel stick with a string)
- Glue
- Online access and printer

Steps

1. Print simple images you find online of actions that the child is working on, such as jumping, running, crawling, or throwing.

2. Attach the picture to the fish with glue or tape. Add a small paper clip to the fish.
3. Have the child go fishing for the paper fish by attaching the magnet at the end of the string to the paper clips on the fish.
4. Have the child complete the action labeled on the fish he catches.

Food painting (fine motor skills)

Kids on the spectrum often require some extra help to practice fine motor skills. Some of the activities involving fine motor skills can be dry and boring. Many kids enjoy the sensation of finger painting, so why not try painting with food? This alternative painting game uses fun things around the house to make painting (and fine motor skills) fun.

Materials

- Finger paint
- Poster board or large sheet of paper
- Painting utensils of different shapes and sizes (for example, vegetable sticks, peas, raisins)

Steps

1. Start with a large painting utensil, such as a vegetable stick.
2. Dip the painting utensil in the finger paint.
3. Suggest the child paint something, such as a house or tree. Depending on the child, you may need to help them paint using hand-over-hand or modeling an image.
4. Begin painting with larger painting utensils (vegetable sticks, leaves) and progress to smaller ones (peas, raisins).

Whack the ball (gross motor skills)

Some kids on the spectrum have difficulties with the basic body coordination needed for sitting, standing, and more. They may lose interest in sports and physical activity or have low self-esteem because of these coordination difficulties. This game is simple and fun, and I've seen many kids use it successfully to build their confidence when playing ball games with other kids.

Whack the ball helps kids develop visual tracking (without the need for video games) and ball skills, and also helps kids with proprioceptive skills (sensory information that contributes to movement and a sense of body position).

But let's not get too technical. It's time to get moving!

Materials

- Balls
- Rope or other hanging spot
- Spandex or panty hose
- Toy baseball bat or paddle

Steps

1. Place the ball in the spandex or panty hose (make sure the ball doesn't fall out).

2. Tie the other end of the spandex or panty hose to a rope suspended between two trees or to any other hanging spot.
3. Have the child hit the ball with the bat or paddle.
4. Adjust the height level if the ball's too easy for the child to reach.

Up and down on the elevator (hand-over-hand gross motor skills)

Many kids on the autism spectrum have a fascination with elevators. In this game, the child makes their own elevator for their toys while they work on gross motor skills and practice the fine art of tying and untying knots (a very useful life skill).

Materials

- Empty tissue box
- Small toys, such as stuffed animals
- String or thin rope
- A place to hang the rope

Steps

1. Cut out one side of the tissue box so that it resembles an elevator car (you may need to help the child).
2. Poke a small hole on one end of the tissue box (the top end of the elevator car).
3. Run the string or thin rope through the hole and have the child tie a knot to fasten the string to the elevator.
4. Put the string or thin rope over a sturdy tree branch or other place.
5. Place a small toy in the elevator car.

6. Have the child pull the toy up in a hand-over-hand motion until it reaches the top. Then have the child slowly bring the elevator back down to the ground.

Alternatives

For older children, have the child tie the string directly onto a stuffed animal (use bigger, heavier stuffed animals). Once the stuffed animal reaches the ground, have the child untie the knot and repeat with another stuffed toy. You can also have the child keep count of how many toys/stuffed animals ride the elevator.

Body coordination activities (bilateral coordination)

Bilateral coordination is needed for use of both sides of the body at one time. Think about basic life skills such as climbing a set of stairs, riding a bicycle, or climbing a ladder. You need both sides of the body to complete these skills. Many children on the autism spectrum need a little more help to develop this type of coordination.

This game helps children develop bilateral coordination. Not only does this help with movement, it also helps children write and learn (both of these activities use both hemispheres of the brain).

Materials

- Hand drum
- Beanbags (optional)
- Coins
- 2 small containers

Steps

1. Drumming — Have the child play the drums by crossing the right hand over the left hand and vice versa.

2. Cross-walk — Have the child walk forward by crossing their left foot over the right food and vice versa while trying to maintain movement in a straight line. Place beanbags on the ground and have the child try to step on

the line of bean bags.

3. Knee-ups — Have the child touch the knee with the opposite hand. Then switch knees. For example, if the child raises the left knee, have the child touch the knee with the right hand. Then have the child raise the right knee and touch the knee with the left hand.

4. Coin toss — Have the child sit on the floor. Place two small containers on the floor, one to the left side of the child and one to the right. Instruct the child to toss the coins, one at a time, using the left hand to toss to the right container and the right hand to toss to the left container.

Core crab walk (stomach exercises)

This activity engages core muscles in the abdomen and back needed for long periods of sitting in the classroom or at home. Without good core development, the child will struggle to sit still for more focused-related tasks. By developing this core group of muscles, you'll find that the endurance of movement and coordination activities also improves.

Materials

- Stretch of floor or grass
- Beanbag or soft toy

Steps

1. Have the child get into the crab-walk position.
2. First, have the child walk backward, and then have the child walk forward. Set a short distance for the child to walk, as this activity can be quite challenging for younger children. As the child becomes more capable of crab walking, increase the distance.
3. Place a beanbag (or soft toy) on the child's stomach and instruct the child to crab walk, keeping the beanbag from falling. Remind the child to make slow and controlled movements rather than racing through the walk.

Alternatives

Use this activity outdoors and create an obstacle course to make it more challenging. Get involved! Try taking turns with the child. This is a great outdoor activity for playdates as well.

About The Author

Catherine Pascuas is an autism specialist and founder of Edx Autism Consulting, providing training and consultation to families and organizations that support individuals with autism. Catherine incorporates her knowledge from 8 years spent working one-on-one with children and consulting with families using Applied Behavior Analysis, SCERTS, and play therapy. She provides in-person workshops as well as online training and long-distance coaching to families.

Catherine is also the producer and host of The Autism Show podcast, a weekly interview show with top autism experts and changemakers (including Temple Grandin, Areva Martin, and Tania Marshall).

Catherine lives in Vancouver and has a family member on the autism spectrum.

Resources

Looking for more fun activities that promote growth for kids on the spectrum?

Here's a list of website resources you may want to take a look at:

Communication:

The Hanen Centre

www.hanen.org

Social Skills:

Social Thinking

www.socialthinking.com

Life Skills:

The Pocket OT

www.pocketot.com

The Autism Show Podcast

Visit The Autism Show website, www.AutismShow.org, for free interviews with autism experts and resources on autism.

You'll find free interviews with the best minds in the field and hear from parents and adults on the autism spectrum. The Autism Show podcast focuses on positivity and progress that individuals on the autism spectrum can achieve.

We are proud to focus and provide resources to help people on the autism spectrum and their families achieve independence, productivity, and happiness.

Kickstarter

Thanks to all our Kickstarter campaign collaborators who helped make the Autism Activities Handbook a reality:

Sarah Gibbon, Jodi Murphy, Kyle Pearce, Carmen, Jason Eads, Lev Agranovich, Alicia Parayno, Megan, Julio Medrano, Niki Dun, Vidhur, Janet Walmsley, Maneesh Puri, Fathi Abdelsalam, Laura Aslan, Ashlyn Prasad, Deanna, Deb Gordon, Shashi, Kathy Kelly, Maddie DiPasquale Rausch, Vanessa Sutton, Brad Ludwig, Alexander, Marcus Chick, Teach Speech Apps, Ben Chutz, Rania, David Robertson, Gemma Scott, Emily Chan, Vive Wong, Kaina Davignon, Sandra Turner, Jean Nicol, Carole Excell, Stephen Abrahams, Ana Lora Garrard, Jeffrey Segal, Caroline McCarthy, Salvador Zinatelli, Dane De Silva, Caique Santiago, Monique Davidoff, Daniela Lopez, Natalia de Sousa, Graham Mcphee, Susan de Sousa, Jeanette Purkis, Jenny Anderson, and Jon D'Alessandro

Silver Backers

RiSE Scholarship Foundation

G. Sandiford

Kim

Kais

Lois Jean Brady and Mathew Guggemos

DayCape app

I Get It! apps

Mendability

Gold Backers

Kozie Clothes (http://www.kozieclothes.com/)

Chewigem (http://chewigem.com/)

Made in the USA
Columbia, SC
23 October 2018